REALMS

P A T R I C I A   G O R M A N

BALBOA.
PRESS
A DIVISION OF HAY HOUSE

Balboa Press books may be ordered through booksellers or by contacting:

Balboa Press
A Division of Hay House
1663 Liberty Drive
Bloomington, IN 47403
www.balboapress.com
1-(877) 407-4847

Because of the dynamic nature of the Internet, any web addresses or links contained in this book may have changed since publication and may no longer be valid. The views expressed in this work are solely those of the author and do not necessarily reflect the views of the publisher, and the publisher hereby disclaims any responsibility for them.

The author of this book does not dispense medical advice or prescribe the use of any technique as a form of treatment for physical, emotional, or medical problems without the advice of a physician, either directly or indirectly. The intent of the author is only to offer information of a general nature to help you in your quest for emotional and spiritual well-being. In the event you use any of the information in this book for yourself, which is your constitutional right, the author and the publisher assume no responsibility for your actions.

Any people depicted in stock imagery provided by Thinkstock are models, and such images are being used for illustrative purposes only.
Certain stock imagery © Thinkstock.

Printed in the United States of America.

ISBN: 978-1-4525-7880-4 (sc)
ISBN: 978-1-4525-7881-1 (e)

Library of Congress Control Number: 2013913581

Balboa Press rev. date: 08/02/2013

Table of Contents

Dedication

This book is dedicated to Tracy, Jim, and John.
The loves of my life.
To Bob my one and only forever.

My six gifts:
Kyle, Colleen, Alex, Tom, Jessica, Laura
my grandchildren.
And to my bonus..great grandchild, Austin.

To Mom, Dad, and Judi
reading from the other side.

Preface

**"In My Fathers house
are many mansions......"
John 14:2**

This small book of poems is meant to depict how we all inhabit many mansions, play many roles, exist in infinite realms. Some of which we haven't recognized yet.

We move through many realms at once ...from the darkest of times to normal events and on to the sublime. Family, nature, death, humor, Spirit, these are our "mansions".

"The Kingdom of heaven is within you." But we continue to search until we end where we started. In the original realm.......HOME.

It is my hope that you will receive inspiration, experience a different point of view, gain understanding, or just have a good laugh. I also hope it deepens the connection between us all and let Love "ignite the spark and fan the flame".

Realms

There is a realm....
so silent you can witness
God imagining
a smooth, gentle hum
of ideas.

There is a realm....
where ideas incubate
in a sacred womb
until thoughts form a mist.

There is a realm....
where ideas
as sparkling droplets
trickle to quench
thirsty minds.

There is a realm....
where thoughts cascading as
waterless falls
pour into
open minds.

There is a realm....
where gossamer words are
too thin to print
too fragile to speak.

There is a realm....
where images consummate
with language and language
with perception and perception
with sentiment.

There is a realm....
where words,
visions and feelings
radiate and solidify.

We inhabit these realms....
and each one of us
carries the gene of silence.

Brilliance

My light shines brilliant
this day
rivaling the sun
Melting all darkness
whose purpose is done.

Brilliance
seeping through my pores
like burning celluloid.
watching forms dissolve
in soft radiant brilliance.

Brilliance
de-intensifies into enlightenment
our brains can accept
without damage.

Brilliance
staring into the sun
blinds the eyes
Too long in the realm of brilliance
blinds us to purpose.

Brilliance
Speak it , feel it.
envision it as
ripples of white
silver satin
waving in the atmosphere.

Brilliance
like diamond
facets reflecting
infinite realms
we inhabit simultaneously.

My light shines brilliant
this day
rivaling the sun
Melting all darkness
whose purpose is done.

Soul Mates

In times of contemplation
if everything seems dark
Remember our creation
when God breathed in the spark.

When Life was given to us
we both became aware
of the stirring of the ethers
and each other being there.

Recall the silent beauty
when everything was still
Feel the Love remaining
and cherish it until

The time we come together
and you'll become aware
of the stirring of your Spirit
and of me being there.

The Unexpected

Now and again
we stumble across something
unexpected....
a face in a flower
a shape in the clouds
snow in the desert
the moon rolling down the mountain.

It is finding God
hiding unannounced
when life surprises us
with a healing
a blessing
an appearance out of nowhere.
I enjoy not expecting
the unexpected.
I watch for it.

Love Was Born on Christmas

I was born to the world on Christmas
but I've existed since the beginning.
I am the gift of God.
I am gift-wrapped
with the soft tender body of a baby.
My ribbons are streams of Divine Light.
I am placed under the tree of Truth
and opened through the seeking of it.
I am received by giving.
I am the Spirit of Christmas.
I am not the carol
but the urge to sing it.
I am not the gift
but the act of giving it.
I am not Bethlehem
but the creation of it.
I am not the world
but the Presence within it.
I am your natural sate of Being.
I am here.
I am now.
I am Love.

Author's note.... In the line I am your natural sate of being, the word "sate" is not a typo.

According to the dictionary, it means to satisfy or fulfill. So Love satisfies and fulfills your Being.

MYSTIC LOVE TRILOGY
I

In this world we are limited
to small blocks of time
to learn of each other......
Yet, there is a world of intimacy.....
a world where Spirits blend
and form invisible bonds.
Our eyes meet
our startled souls
rejoice in recognition
Our love
draws its first breath.
Have I awakened a part of you?
Am I part of you?
a part you were ready to meet?

I gaze into your Spirit
and see my reflection there.
How beautiful you are
how beautiful
you make me feel.
My Love...How enchanted I am
in your presence
How blessed you are
in my heart.

II

You broke through
emotional barriers
You scaled walls
set up for my protection
You planted the seed
of our love
in the garden
of my heart.

It took root in the fertile soil
of your caring nature
It grew with intensity
in the sacred elements of beauty and trust
nourished by the sunlight
of your smile
watered by soft showers of
tears and laughter.
Now it stands....
a flower..strong and gentle
a living Love
for all to see.

III

Love is born
at the moment of Creation
and seeks itself
throughout Infinity.
Our time was eons ago...
Our time is eternity
in the best of all worlds.
We are woven together
with threads of consciousness
never to unravel.

Love...
how beautiful the word
My Love...
how enchanted I am
in your presence...
How blessed you are
in my heart.

The Bird

A bird flew into a valley surrounded by mountains.
He flew to the North but there blocking his way was a
majestic mountain.
He veered to the East but there blocking his way was a
a majestic mountain.
He veered to the South but there blocking his way was another
majestic mountain.
He veered to the West but there again was a
majestic mountain.
He flew again to the North and at the base
of the mountain
sat a Holy One in a state of perfect serenity.
The Wise One watched
calmly as the bird flew round and round trying to
escape his mountain prison.
The bird finally perched
on the Holy Ones' finger and said,
"Master, kindly show
me the way out – I have been flying around for such a long
time."
The Holy One looked kindly upon the bird and whispered,
"Fly higher."

The Coming of the Monsoon

The desert air is dry...
as dry as the tongue of the arroyo
begging for just one lap of river
screaming for a rush of water
"Just this once..
I'll never ask again".

Twirling sand devil scurries
across the desert floor.
"I have no water..
but, I'll give you what life I have"
it says.

The saguaro stretches its arms
reaching toward the sky
poking....pleading
"I'm almost empty...
is there nothing for me?"

The sky in the distance is slate blue
lightning dances over the mountains
like live electrical wires.
Rejoice, you dying desert...
prepare to meet your heaven
drop
  by
    drop.

Once Upon a Desert Night

John and I sat out
sky watching
shaping the clouds
with the fingers of our minds
counting the silver javelins
streaking through the sky
piercing the darkness
like sparkle-tipped arrows.
Stars twinkling to the rhythm of the crickets
shaking their jingle bells
never ending bells
no intermission.
The Big Dipper pours white lava
down the mountain side
while the moon plays close to home.
Coyotes howl a warning to
the creatures of the dark
"It's time to take refuge
the night is mine."
John and I take heed
and head for home
stealing one last look
one last listen
before dawn
paints over the picture.

Fog in the Desert

Now and again
I wake up
to a foggy mountain
morning
When the fog is
close to the ground
It slides along
stealthy as snake
Rising
obscuring vision.
Just as in life
we see fog
but not beyond.
When fog is
born high
It appears as mist
crawling over
The mountain
spilling silently
down the other side.
Just as in life
we see fog
also mountains
through a blur of mist
but not beyond.

Mother Autumn

Mother Autumn gently stroking
  summers fevered brow
Rocking her to sleep
  with a cool evening sigh
Placing on a blanket of
  red and green and gold
Orange harvest moon
    keeping vigil in the sky.

Gathering her offspring
  colors to her breast
Tearfully preparing
  summers tomb
Contented suckling colors
  she lays them to their rest
Awaiting birth of winter
  from her swelling womb.

Drawing in the slowly dying
  summers final breath
She promises to cherish
  summers' dreams
Breathing life into the infant
  winters' blessed scene
She's the sacred meeting place
  of two extremes.

Indian Flute

Day---
   Sweet echo
   life beckoning life
   arising, gliding
   on the back of
   a woodwind bird
   warbling melodies
   awaken the sun
   generate the
   shimmering stream.

Night---
   Haunting echo
   spirit summoning spirit
   night breeze carries
   sacred breath whispering
   through the song of
   a woodwind bird
   fluttering wings
   generate the
   twinkling stars.

Creation becomes a silhouette on the moon.

Since I Left

Tucked under the open sky
night moves all around me –
  covers me like a velvet hood.
No one hears my muffled cries.
Something scurries – howls.
Leaves tremble – startled by a sudden breeze.
Air circles and spirals –
Hugging my form.
Everything moves but the blood in my veins.
I remain still –
  scar tissue forms.

Sister Jude

I

My sister Judi is dying
She is leaving us in this world
  of unending forms
where we believe only what we see.
Soon she'll be as a tree in winter
  that's shed its leaves.
It appears to have no life.
But appearances deceive.

Silent Life prepares for Spring
  formulating invisible leaves...
  buds..
  blossoms...
  fruit...
We don't see.
Does it know?
I think it knows.

It will be like that
  when God awakens Sister Jude.
We'll remain in dreams
  and won't see while her life
continues unmeasured by Winters and Springs.

She is so much a part of our Soul
  she will live as silently in us
as the life lives in the tree
despite its barrenness.

Even now, there is a Presence,
  Pure
  Sharp
  Keen
guiding her through.
Does she know?
I think she knows.

II

Will we feel her?
Will we see her in our children?
  and in theirs?
In familiar
places,
  faces,
    sounds,
    things?
She will be there smiling, shining
  with the shrug of a shoulder
    a wink of an eye
      a certain inflection
        in a special word
Letting us know.
Will we know?
I think we'll know.
When God awakens
  Sister Jude.

Sister

You were my sister
we shared our lives.
I the older "nice" one
you the younger daredevil
separate lives bound by love.
I there for you
you there for me.

You were at your best
when your time came.
You looked up to me as a child.
I looked up to you when you faded
so eloquently brave.

Never saw you so strong.
Never felt so weak...helpless.
I said you were my sister.
You still are.

You just moved inside.

Some Say She's an Angel

Some say she's an angel
  now
Holy, Sacred, dressed in white.
  but to me she's just
  my sister
Just as she's always
  been.

Funny, smiling, listening to
  music.
Taking in cats
  playing with children,
Laughing, laughing,
  laughing
Mostly at us.

I see her
  when I want...
closing my eyes
  she's here
trying to tell us
  It's all good
with her.

I still feel her
  looking over my shoulder
  making me laugh
Singing along with
  the Beatles.

They can believe she's an angel
  whatever helps them
  cope.
As for me....
She's still
  just my sister
  she's here
  I love her.

21

Perception

I look toward Ireland
and see my fathers' eyes
smiling sad, filled
with visions and revisions.

Uillean pipes
echo my fathers' cries
unrehearsed miracles spilling
out more life than expected.

Shades of green
reflect my fathers' moods
intense and bright shadows
rooted in the grave.

In the simple shamrock
my father lives frightened
and free – the meadow
has no walls.

No longer an island
my father transforms
assimilates an ocean of spirit
no longer alone.

Just So You Know…
(reflections on my mothers' death)

I slept on the night
  you died—
for a while
Next days' flight was
  unsettling.
I looked down on the world
  you just left
It looked up at me and smiled—
I cried.

I wish I were a child
  again
believing people lived in the sky
  sitting on clouds
  chatting with God.
I find myself looking out
  at each cloud –hoping to see you.

I stayed at your house
  slept in your bed
  thought maybe
  I would see a shadow..
  feel a presence..
You were gone.

I waded through your possessions
  wondering if I would find a part of you
  I didn't know...
Or a part of me
  long forgotten.

I wore your clothes
  to your funeral..
Do I hear you laugh?

The weather was
  never better
The luncheon was fine.
They misspelled your name
I was annoyed
  They should take better care.

We didn't go to your grave
  frozen ground
We left you in your coffin
  in the chapel.
It was white—
  your coffin
nice looking—
  very chic.
You'd approve.
It broke my heart
  just broke my heart
    to leave you there.

Back at your house
  children running, playing
  neighbors with food
  kind words
Memories exploding
  from every corner
  from every mind
  from every heart.
How could you die
  right in the middle of all this life?

I found a little tablet
  blank pages
  except for one.
"It's hard to hear
  when hate keeps shouting
    in your ear."
Your handwriting.
I didn't say anything to anyone
I just took it—
  it's all I wanted....
It came from your heart.

To "the Bear"

You first came to us under protest
  My protest.
I did not want a dog
  I did not.
For years I put my foot down
  Dogs are dirty
  Dogs smell
  Dogs need a lot of care.
But, eventually, four against one
Amid promises
  "I'll walk him."
  "I'll give him a bath."
  "I'll take care of him."
I lifted my foot for a split second
  You snuck in.

One by one they left
  To their own lives
There we were
  You, me and Dad.
I walked you
  I bathed you
I took care of you
  And I loved you.
Memories pop up
  Like ducks in a row
I'm not ready to shoot them down.
The way you loved that bath...
  How excited you were when you saw me
  Put on my "dog washin' shoes"...
The jingle of the tags on your leash
  Sent you into a frenzy.
The baby talk....
  "You're the best dog in the world
   the only dog I love
     You're my best, best boy, Bear."

I swear I saw you smile.
You loved being brushed.
  How many hours did I brush?
I knew every bone in your body
  Every bump.
You looked so handsome
  And shiny...
I can still feel your fluff even now
  This moment.
The palms of my hands tingle
  As they glide over your fur
  In my minds' eye.

You were there for me
Someone to love
  When I felt unloved.
Someone to mother
  When my children were gone
Someone to touch
  When I needed to touch.
You were my silent partner
  For all these years.
You shared my laughter
  My tears.
You watched with me
  As my grandchildren were born
  Into this world.
You watched with me
  When my parents were born
  Into eternity.
My walking partner
  My audience
You were there.
  You were there.
  You were there.

Dr. Edwards said,
  "You have a decision to make."
I felt a tear in my heart
I couldn't let you go—
I couldn't see you in pain.
I couldn't bear to see you in pain, Bear.

As a final act of love
I sat on the floor cross-legged
Cupped my hands
  And held them out to you
    As I had done thousands of times before.
You put your head in my hands
  As you had done thousands of times before.
With Dad patting your back----
I stared into your eyes
  As the needle went in---
"You're the best dog in the world
  The only dog I love
    You're my best, best boy, Bear
      And I love you."
I swear I saw you smile.
You closed your eyes
  And for a split second
    I wanted to change my mind.
Your head tilted just a touch
  And you were gone
    Quick, peaceful, and final.

13 years of love came pouring out
  of my eyes
    and my heart.
I ran my hands along your back
  I knew every bone—
    Every bump
I wiped my tears
  And cleaned your eyes with them.
I'm heartbroken
  Just heartbroken
I'm unashamed of that.
The scene plays and replays
  The tear in my heart goes deeper.
I miss you.
  I miss you.
    I miss you.

If God has any mercy,
  On some level
You are aware of the great purpose
  You played in my life
And how much you are loved.

This House

This is the hallway where
he used to stop me
  on my way to our room
  with an armful of laundry.
He would grab me
and kiss me and laugh
when I tried to pull away.

This is the cabinet that held
our favorite dishes
  that one cereal bowl that
  made everything taste just right...
The glass that held
 just the right amount...
the cutting board Jim made in woodshop...
the cup John made in the kiln in 4th grade
  and here is the pin cushion Tracy
  made in sewing class....
  or was it Campfire Girls?

They grew up here....
they experienced all the good and bad
that children go through.
I grew up here too....
and had to experience all things adult.

I never thought it would be so painful to leave.
I didn't realize the memories
  would be so strong....
like threaded needles piercing my skin
  stinging when I try to pull away.

I can't bear the empty front room
  that was once the hub of activity.
How many games did we play here?
How many conversations did we have?
How many friends came and went here?

But most of all, I'll
miss this room.
this room where we shared our most
private moments.
This room
where our children used to run in and jump
 in our bed on Sunday morning.
This room
where everyone came
  at one time or another
to be alone.
How much of ourselves are we leaving here?
the secrets it could tell.
One last look....
Sadness lays on me
like a heavy blanket on a
summer day.
I can't think about the echo of
the closing door.
Always, always, there will be
an aching in my heart for
this house.

Family
Rise and Fall

Eight of us in the
  house we shared.
The goings on of
  a typical family.
Laugh, cry, anger, fight,
  hurt, give , take, adjust,
Start another day
  then someone moves away.

Each one different
  learning to
integrate, celebrate, create, and
  God help us procreate.
Dinner at five
  like bees in a hive
table cleared
  dishes done.

Marriage, children
  expand, understand,
disband, demand,
  command.
Then the back bone breaks
  unknown fates
Poppy flew to heaven
Then there were seven.

Together to grieve
  begin to weave
a new bond to stretch
  leaving the nest.
Throw a few more kids
  in the mix
Aunnie dies
And then there were six.

Six adult children
  on with their lives
 keeping in touch
  a family survives
Hearts breaking as one
  together alone
Judi dies
And then there were five.

Five grieving
  each in their way
There own memories
  to keep and to say
Wondering who will
  be next to depart
Leaving the grieving
  behind them to start

New families
  keep them close
If not forever
  forever almost.

The Music Box

Just a little music box
tinkling in the night
on top there stood a lady
dressed in blue and white.

I found it in a little shop
just outside of Rome
It reminded me of Mama
and a little house back home.

It played Ave Maria
which was her favorite song
I knew just when I heard it
I had been gone too long.

I traveled all around the world
from the Delta lands to Nome
while Mama sat there waiting
waiting all alone.

Arriving at the airport
I promptly hailed a cab
then noticed that the little town
was still so dull and drab.

I walked into the little house
my suitcase in my hand
Mama was asleep in bed
a rosary in her hand.

I placed the box right next to her
just beside her head
I kissed her on the cheek
and then I went to bed.

Mama passed away that night
before the morning light
I swear I'd heard that music box
tinkling in the night.

If I live to be one hundred
I won't forget that sound
of the pretty little music box
and the lady turning 'round.

A Memory

Late autumn afternoon—
smell of burning leaves against the curb
Big finale for the day long workout—
Leaves, leaves
crunching, crackling
wet and cold
raking and rolling
Jumping into piles only to start again.

Crisp, cold air – nose running
How I loved that red jacket.
Hours of agony – combing leaf fragments
out of my braids.
Glow from the kitchen window
Steak night, home-made French fries.

Nothing comes to mind – nothing
that compares to the warmth and contentment
and feeling of well-being on that
Late autumn afternoon.

Meloncholia

I am sitting cross-legged
in the palms of Gods cupped hands
supporting my chin with my fist
talking about my mood.

When I'm like this—
  I see no reason or pattern –
    everything out of sync
When I'm like this –
  I hang from a thread of sanity
Like a spider dangling
  from the ceiling
Little by little –
  I lower myself, never sure of
Where I am
  or what will happen until
I touch bottom
Bottomed out, depressed, desperate
  then five minutes later –
    by the clock in the kitchen
I'm skimming the fuzz
  off the clouds.

"So, what part of Catholicism
  are you from?" God asks.
"Hmmm – let me think about that", says I.

I dreamt my father was on fire
  I grabbed a hose and put him out.
He kept walking back into the fire
  I lived with a hose at arms' reach.
When he went in for the last time
  we buried him with his ice cream napkin
Last I heard
  he was living in a Bing Crosby movie.
Now Mom is talking about the lure of flames
and I live with fear at arms reach.

"Altitude dementia", says God.
"What?"
"Altitude dementia", says God.
"You're climbing higher and the air is thinner
    and you're forced to leave some memories
    behind. They get a bit heavy.
You get to a certain point and the 'ol memory tree becomes desolate
– stricken with blight. The past is swallowing itself and all who live
in it are shaking their heads crying,
"The river doesn't live here anymore."

"Hey, that's pretty good", says I.
"I see what you mean".

I used to pick memories
  like cherries off a tree
leaving behind the bruised
  and broken.

The older ones are all going now
  taking their rosary beads with them
    clutched in their bony fingers –
giving up their houses –
  they're all giving up their houses –
and, yes, pushing me up
    one rung on the ladder.
Jesus!

"Yes?"

"Oh, sorry – I didn't mean that literally."

"It's OK. Don't let it happen again. I'm much too
busy closing chapters and dismantling the night
sky. The day's about to begin."

"I didn't realize familiarity is such a gift.
I didn't notice it dissipating – I was too
busy NOT closing chapters."

"Very good", says God. I'm happy you learned
something. Now let's start this day –
Ready
Set
Don't forget to take your estrogen!"

"Thanks, God, but don't get too excited –
I wouldn't want you to clap your hands!",
Says I.

Butterfly
For Yvonne

Remember the butterfly......
He came to visit when I came to visit.
We laughed at the persistence shown...
The strength, the confidence........
Demanding we pay attention to its beauty
Teaching us about struggle and freedom and gentle rest.

I remember that butterfly ....
As I remember you.
I marvel at how we mimic Nature.....
How we persist, use our inner strength,
  develop our confidence
    but seldom pay attention to our beauty.
We struggle for freedom and gentle rest.

I remember your words.........
"All I need is sleep...I'll be fine if I can sleep"
You are so close now in your chrysalis stage.
You struggle for freedom over and over......
You emerge from your cocoon to fly strong
To light on a heavenly leaf and warm yourself
In the center of the sun.
Sleep a gentle sleep tonight, my friend
For tomorrow you begin new life.

Images of the Holocaust

victims of mutant minds
"" disbandsion of family
wave after wave

      familial forms reflected in
      the eyes – gone with a blink-
      reappear in a stare.

The Cosmic strobe flashes again and again.

screaming souls
hanging like fringe
from a sleeve

      gossamer faces
      imprinted on smoke
      in a charred sky.

The Cosmic strobe flashes again and again.

flames leaping
licking the feet
of angels

      morsels in the mouths of ovens
      death in its darkest form
      sinking deeper and deeper into the Presence of God

The Cosmic strobe flashes again and again.

illegality of dreams
mutilation of flesh
at the mercy of translation

sweet cry of a
violin escaping
from the back of a throat.

The Cosmic strobe flashes again and again.

It tries to fade but –

images of the unreal
reality stomping through
the streets of the mind

the torment of a memory
and the wail of a broken heart
startles her back.

And the Cosmic strobe flashes again and again and again and
again....................

The Phone Call

Shrill intruder violates silence
wrenching you from the warmth
of my arms.

With much effort, I peel the sleep paint
pry the heavy-lidded windows of my eyes
and peer through the slats.

You, hopping on one foot, then the other
struggling like a snake crawling
back into its skin.

Whooshing denim and dull
thuds growing fainter
raspy, slurred irritation.

I grope for the sheet pulling
it to my neck – skin unclenching
satisfied – the shiver is foiled again.

Too contented to laugh – a smile
pours over me like warm honey.
Again I pry and peer.

You shed your denim skin.
Wrong number?
Come, join me in my cocoon.

Mother Ireland

If you close your eyes and listen
there's a voice that you can hear
Tis' softer than the harp strings
that whisper in your ear
It spoke to me in Ireland
from every stream and glen
from famine fields and bog lands
from mountains to the sea
The voice that cries---
My children
Come home again to me.

It's in the rushing waters
that pound the Cliffs of Mohr
It's in the tears of Belfast
and every Dublin door
It's in the Glens of Antrim
each brick in Derry's wall
The voice of Mother Ireland
gives a pleading call
The voice that cries---
My children
Come home again to me.

Her womb no longer barren
Her spirit bright and strong
She beckons to her children
to join her in her song
From the lakes of old Killarney
from the Isle of Innisfree
from the Castle at Blarney
to the rushing Irish Sea
The voice that cries...
My children
Come home again to me.

Chicago Christmas

Every year at Christmas time
my mind is magnetized
I watch the images and scenes
unfold before my eyes.
Childhood scenes that warm my heart
and leave me all aglow
Chicago Christmas images
as they begin to flow.

The wonder windows at State Street Fields
the Water Tower in lights
green wreaths - red bows
on street light poles
the city wrapped in white
reflections of two lovers
in the window of Tiffanys
Chicago Christmas calls me home
to join the jubilee.

The slapping sound of hurried feet
 as snow turns into slush
Salvation Army thank you's
to shoppers in their rush.
The strains of Christmas music heard
in every flake of snow
The cold Chicago Christmas
is the warmest thing I know.

The wonder window at State Street Fields
the Water Tower in lights
green wreaths - red bows
on street light poles
the city wrapped in white reflections of two lovers
in the window of Tiffanys
Chicago Christmas calls me home
to share the jubilee.

I'll always have these memories
no matter where I go
the cold Chicago Christmas
is still the warmest thing I know.

The Christmas Glow

When you stare at the lights
  on a Christmas tree
your eyes go slightly
  out of focus....
You will see a warm glow
  surrounding each light.
It's Gods' way of softening
  the harshness.

It's so "Christmas"
  when that glow surrounds
each and every being
  and filters out the glare
of the human condition.
We can share the peaceful softness
  of our Spiritual essence
and feel the warmth of the World
  within our world.

Damn Cricket!

Damn cricket!
I see you –
  out of the corner of my eye
I try to write but
  there you are.
Intruding – distracting – vying for my attention.
Now where are you?
You've disappeared from view.

Damn cricket!
I know you're lurking – ready to spring
To make me
  gasp
To take me
  away from
  my task.
I know you're hiding
  in the pile of clothes.
I pick them up – one by one
  tense, holding my breath
  give them a shake
    preparing for the surprise.

Damn cricket!
Now that you have my undivided—
Where are you?
You've disappeared from view.
You've crawled into the pages of my book
  haven't you?
A quick fling – Bang!
  against the wall
Pages fanning
  it falls.

Damn cricket! Where are you?
You've disappeared from view.
Ah, yes, you're in my shoe
I pick it up – looking for you.
But what's this I see?

Black cricket – white wall.
I raise my shoe
  ready to
    strike at last.
but, alas—
It's something I cannot do.

Damn cricket!
  Shoo!
Disappear from view!

The Dentist

She decided after 20 years
It was time for her to face her fears.
"Do a good job,
and don't be shoddy,
it's the second most sensitive
part of my body".
The tooth man said, "I'll do no harm
Then pulled out a needle
as long as her arm.
He injected the liquid
into her gum
The tip of the needle reached
her eardrum.
Then he tugged and he pulled
with all his might
"I don't understand why
this is so tight."
He paused several times
to wipe his brow
"Oh, I do believe
it's coming now".
She let out with
a feeble moan
for attached to the tooth
was a section of bone
And attached to the bone
was her upper lip
a portion of kidney
and her lower right rib.
And attached to her rib
was a disc from her spine
her remaining lip quivered
and she started to whine.

For attached to the disc
was her bottom left lung
and she winced as she felt
a slight tug on her tongue.
"I really must tell you
this is quite rare,
I must show my partner
I really must share."
"Let me make sure
I have it all."
And she watched her parts
trail him down the hall.
Her body was weak
and wracked with pain
as he said, "Well, good-bye,
come see us again.
And here take your tooth
with my warmest regards."
"Sorry", she said,
"it won't fit in the car!"

The Librarian and the Mouse

Deep, deep in the dark corner
lies the cold and baited trap
Awaiting the arrival of the small gray guest
The sniff, the bite, the snap!

She tiptoed in as dawn approached
the rodent to extract
To her surprise, the cheese was gone
the trap was still intact.

Every morn as dawn approached
she came to check the trap
And every day the bait was gone
with no sign of mishap.

Then one fine day the plan was set
the sticky glob in place
honey, nuts and raisins
in a peanut butter base.

No need to tiptoe in today
She boldly took her steps
and made her way across the room
to where the trap was kept.

She smiled and sighed at what she saw
her suspicions were correct.
His snout was stuck in the glob
the bar behind his neck.

Up and down she jumped with glee
Her joy had reached its peak
She almost wished she could have heard
his shocked and muffled squeak.

Her joy was spent, she sat alone
surprised at what she felt
a feeling of accomplishment
without a twinge of guilt.

I know I really should feel bad
I know I really should
But would I do it all again?
Would I? You bet I would!

To a Cow on a Winters Day

It happened at the old Dude Ranch
 in a town in Illinois
To a small group of children
a field trip to enjoy.

They ran across the snow filled field
As pure as their innocence
One little lass with bright red hair
Climbed on a wooden fence.

Her bulging eyes and hanging tongue
revealed she was in awe
A bony little finger raised
to point at what she saw.

"Hey, you guys, come here", she said
"Don't worry, it's quite safe."
One by one they made their way
and gathered 'round the waif.

Several of them climbed the fence
Each exclaiming, "Wow!"
For safely on the other side
was a big old milking cow.

The big round eyes stared straight ahead
It's hair as smooth as silk.
On her underside the pouch
that once had given milk.

There's something you should know
about this cow", she said.
It's stiff legs reaching toward the sky
"The gosh darn thing is dead."

"Ooh, ick! Oh yuk!", the children cried
all quite theatrical
"We should have a service
for our frozen Cowsicle."

"Here lies Bossy in her home
and may she rest in peace
and take her to Cow Heaven, Lord
too bad she had to freeze."

"But in the summer, she'll thaw out
and the flies will eat a bunch
Come on, guys, we better go
I think it's time for lunch".

Forest in Need of Rain

The life that once called
the creek home..
Is still here...
somewhere.

Dead branches stand out
draped across the blue sky.
How many dimensions superimposed
by Natures' camera?
Branches...all kinds
Branches that look
like shepherds' staff
Branches to climb
like circular ladders
Branches peeling like
grass skirts or
New Years Eve streamers.

Cones sleeping on their mattress
of pine needles.
Violets and dandelions
as live as can be
foretelling life ready
to spring forth
in this
Forest in need of rain.

Forest Walk at Winters' End

I came today
It's sunny, cool, windy
I came to see
  what toll winter had taken.
Tree sticks—toothpicks
Sacred leaf fasteners
  outliving their purpose
thrown into the air.
They land every which-way
  a giant game of pick-up sticks.

How cruel winter can be...yet how beautiful.
Nothing is as warm as a snow-covered tree.
Nothing is as cold as the grey-brown refuse
  winter leaves behind.

I walk along taking inventory.
One tree missing here—two have fallen over there.
Fallen heroes
  one on top of the other.
I hear it even now.
Yet, how silently
  they must have fallen
under the weight of the cotton snow.
I take a deep breath.
Crisp, cool, the sun is warm.
there is something in the air.
Spring?

Nature's Playground

I love trees
  that have spaces
where light darts around leaves
  playing hide and seek
  changing shape
  branch to branch

I love leaves
  that twirl and spin
intent on forcing light
  into movement
  teaching it to
    hop
    skip
    jump

I love branches
  stretched over sky
breaking into segments
  divining
  defining
  designing

The tree poses
  silent and still
  a playground
  for Nature.

Night and Eve

Coyote owns the desert night
He fills the silence with his song
None else lays claim to desert night
So to none else does it belong.

But I stake claim to sunsets all
Abalone or crimson red
The soft brushed skies of desert eve
Lay as a quilt on the desert bed.

The Spoilers

Her rock has crumbled into powder
  Her desert is filled with shattered glass
Her birds are stumbling across the sky
  Her moon is missing from the sea.

Who has raped Mother Earth?
She screams for mercy
  but no one hears.
They entered through the back door
  and stole her beauty out from under us.
The Spoilers.

Her virginity is lost but once
  yet they violate her again
and again while our heads
  are turned and our eyes
are blind from staring too long
  at the sun.

Her sky rains people
  and her oceans choke on the darkness.
Her pores are clogged with plastic
  and she is tattooed with dollar signs.

Now she begins Her menopausal journey.
she'll be barren soon
  and we shall feel her
tremble and hear
  the rattle of death in her throat.
We all must see—
We all must feel—
We all must save her from
The Spoilers.

Jewels of Nature

Have you ever seen the jewels
Nature tries to hide?
They give the world its' beauty
abundantly supplied.
They most often go unnoticed
In the worries of the day
But the sparkling gems of Nature
shine forth in full array.

There is gold within the sun
silver in the rain
emeralds in the grass
amber in the grain.
Clouds of pearl suspended
in the blue sapphire sky
that cause the ruby in the rose
to blossom with a sigh.

When winter comes upon us
and life has ceased to grow
don't be so blind as not to see
the diamonds in the snow.
There's crystal in the icicles
frozen in secure
that give us all a chance to see
a world so clean and pure.

There is gold within the sun
silver in the rain
emeralds in the grass
amber in the grain.
Clouds of pearl suspended
in the blue sapphire sky
that cause the ruby in the rose
to blossom with a sigh.

Peonies

I wonder if the peonies bloomed today
  at the old house.
The ants worked for weeks preparing
  for this day.

Memorial Day - every year
without fail - the peonies bloomed
  at the old house.

It's the only house we ever owned.
  and the only one we ever lost.
It breaks my heart to think the peonies will bloom
  without me.

I hope whoever lives there now notices
  that the peonies bloom on Memorial Day.
Not a day before
  and every day for weeks.

They stay for a while
  not here and gone - like us.
The peonies bloom on Memorial Day
  at the old house.
At least, they still do for me.

Daily Prayer

Father of the Universe
and all who dwell within
its infinity,
Express through me this day
Your Grace.
Reveal Your plan to awaken
us to Your Presence.

Let me give and give and
keep on giving until
Your Love ignites the spark in
every being
and let me fan the flame.

About the Author

Patricia Gorman is the mother of three, grandmother of six and a great grandmother. She works a full time job and writes poetry in her spare time.

After her first poem was published, she extended the proverbial bucket list to making Christmas cards using her poems which she has done for the last four years. Next on the list was publishing this book of some of her favorite poems. Next? On to Graceland!

Originally from Chicago, Patricia now lives in Tucson, Arizona with her husband of 49 years, Bob.